LOST AT SEA
FOUND IN HEAVEN
The ARTHUR TAYLOR Story

LOST AT SEA
FOUND IN HEAVEN

The ARTHUR TAYLOR Story
As told to BOB CRETNEY

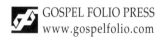

GOSPEL FOLIO PRESS
www.gospelfolio.com

LOST AT SEA, FOUND IN HEAVEN
The Arthur Taylor Story
Copyright © 2005
By Bob Cretney

Published by
GOSPEL FOLIO PRESS
304 Killaly Street West
Port Colborne, ON L3K 6A6

ISBN 1-897117-23-X

Ordering Information:
GOSPEL FOLIO PRESS
Phone: 1-800-952-2382
E-mail: orders@gospelfolio.com
www.gospelfolio.com

Printed in the United States of America

Contents

Acknowledgments

For many years in my travels around Southern Ontario and into the United States, I have been told, "Arthur, you should write a book. Your real-life illustrations make the Bible come alive to me." I always enjoy relating my experiences in conversations as well as from the pulpit. However, when people would say this should be in print, I would always respond that I was too busy and that I didn't have the gift of writing.

When my good friend, Bob Cretney, first approached me about this book, I was truly hesitant. I didn't want people to get the impression that I thought I was important enough to be the subject of a book. As I considered this further, it occurred to me that maybe the Lord could use such a writing to benefit others and I gave him the go ahead to put my feeble words into a more readable print. I realized it could be a tool for the Lord to use for evangelism and for the encouragement of Christians.

I want to thank, and give credit to Bob for persisting in this endeavour and bringing it to a successful conclusion. My prayer is that you will be blessed as you read what GOD can do with an imperfect servant who sometimes uses imperfect methods to share the greatest news in the world— that people can know for sure that they can go to Heaven when they die.

My gratitude also goes out to Bob's son, Brian Cretney, who spent many hours editing the manuscript. As well, my appreciation to Bob's nephew, John Nicholson, who put much time and effort into preparing the pages and cover for the actual printing.

ARTHUR TAYLOR

Foreword

I first met Arthur Taylor in 1972. I was still in university, married, and my wife was expecting our first child. The landlord of our apartment told us we had to leave, because the apartment did not allow children. Our finances were very low and we really could not afford to hire movers. Arthur somehow heard of our situation and told us not to worry— he would get some "guys" from our chapel and have us moved in no time. He was true to his word! What was a stressful situation for my family turned out to be a real blessing. Though we saved on moving expenses, the real treasure was the beginning of a lifelong bond with a dear servant of God, Mr. Arthur Taylor.

It has become obvious to me and to all who know him that Art is a "man after God's own heart." He is committed to the preaching of the gospel, helping those who are in need, and building up believers in the Lord. He has done this, not for self-promotion, but for the praise and glory of God. It was my conviction that his remarkable life story should be in print so that others, too, might be blessed to see how God is willing to do extraordinary things through ordinary believers who are simply available to be used. I approached Arthur with this desire and he agreed.

Lost at Sea, Found in Heaven is a book that will warm your heart and, at times, make you laugh. However, the real value of this book is that it points us to the one true Life Preserver. To all those souls, tossed and troubled on the sea of life, this story will teach you what the fishermen friends of Jesus learned long ago in the stormy waves: It is only when Christ is allowed to be the Captain of our lives that we experience true peace. For, after He took full control of the vessel, *"there was a great calm"* (Matthew 8:23-27).

BOB CRETNEY
ST. CATHARINES, ONTARIO
NOVEMBER, 2005

Introduction

*L*ost *At Sea, Found In Heaven* is the remarkable story of Arthur Taylor of the Welland Canal Mission. Chaplain Taylor is only the fourth missionary to be called by God for a lifetime of service to honour His Name in this unique work.

As you read Arthur's personal story, you will be gripped by God's touch on this humble servant. From his seafaring background to his preparation for ministry, the Lord has clearly brought Arthur to the Welland Canal in a compelling way to serve sailors, their families, and Seaway workers. Arthur has been at work now for 33 years and counting.

As the representative of the Welland Canal Mission, Arthur serves as its Chaplain to Great Lakes and overseas sailors who, by the very nature of their work, are not able to attend regular worship services. Theirs is a seven-day-a-week job, so they are away from home for long periods of time.

The Mission dates back to 1868, and it is an amazing fact that only four men have served as Chaplain in the past 137 years. Each man has worked faithfully for the full term of his ministry.

The Welland Canal Mission is a non-denominational work. It is governed by a Board of Directors that provides direction, encouragement, and oversees the financial stewardship of the Mission. All Board members serve on a completely volunteer basis. We believe that God has met, and continues to meet, all our needs as we rely on Him through prayer, not through appeals to sailors or other individuals for our ongoing support.

Arthur has always been a storyteller and able to weave God's message into his real life experiences. He has touched numerous lives, both on and off the ships, through one-on-one conversations, church services, and missionary conferences. His life and ministry have been marked by times of great joy and great trial; some of these experiences have been captured in this book by Arthur and author, Bob Cretney.

Our prayer is that readers will be enriched and enlightened by reading about Arthur's journey of faith and ministry. This Niagara area mission has sailors from all over the world coming to our doorsteps where they can hear the Good News of the Bible and of God's love for them. We're thankful that Arthur is here waiting for them.

E.B. "SKIP" GILLHAM
PRESIDENT,
WELLAND CANAL MISSION BOARD

CHAPTER ONE

Death at Sea

The last words that my dad ever said to me were, "Cast off the lines, Arthur." My last words to him were, "Don't come back until you catch forty thousand pounds of haddock," a full boat load. He put the boat into gear and we waved good-bye. I watched his boat, the *Muriel Eileen* [1], go out the harbour and disappear behind an island. I would never see him again.

The last day I spent with my father remains vivid in my memory, as though it were yesterday and not forty-four years ago. I still choke up once in awhile when I'm telling the story.

I was fourteen years old and my dad had just made

eggnog for our family breakfast. He leaned up against the stove, hugging my mother, while he sipped his 'nog' and got warm. Dad and I snuck into the pantry and each had a piece of Mom's home-made coconut custard pie, grinning as we enjoyed every bit of it. We then left to cross the frozen pond with axe and bucksaw in hand to cut some skids for my grandfather, who was affectionately known as Grampy. His slip, which is a boat ramp, had washed away in a March gale the week before.

I went with Dad as he consulted Grampy about the weather reports. After Dad gave his mom a hug and a kiss good-bye, our next stop was up at his brother Mitchell's place. He, like my father, was a boat captain. They discussed the weather conditions and the pos-sibility of heading out for the first fishing trip of the season. They were anxious to get started as money was getting scarce and captains couldn't receive unemployment benefits during the winter season. Between my dad and his brother, they had thirteen children who depended on them for support.

The decision was made to go and consult with the other captains at the government wharf in Lockeport. Weather was a major concern for fishermen. Storms came up fast. The high waves could wash over the boat and, with the cold temperature, ice would form on the ship. With no heating system on board, this would make the situation perilous. If the waves broke the windshield, water could also get into the boat's engine room, causing the motor to stall and leaving the men stranded in a boat drifting parallel with the waves—a sailor's nightmare.

We stopped at the fuel dock for water and diesel fuel, just in case. After some discussion, the captains decided to go. While Dad rounded up his crew, I helped load the boat with ice, food, bait and tubs of trawl line. After our final conversation and I saw him sail away, I turned and walked up to the high school where I joined my junior basketball team-mates in a game. Nothing would prepare me for the shocking news that would soon shatter my world.

1. The *Muriel Eileen* was my dad's fifty-three foot fishing long-liner that he named after his wife and her sister.

CHAPTER TWO

Shattered Lives

Everything seemed normal until a few days later. After my brothers and I got off the school bus, we began laughing and goofing around as usual. My grandmother, Nanny, opened the door and yelled at us: "What are you laughing about? They just found your father's boat awash at sea, with the wheel house missing and no sign of the men." I was stunned into silence. I wondered, "Was it that ferocious winter storm that went through our town the other day?"

All seven of us children were quiet around the supper table when Mom burst out, "Poor Lawrence!" She started to cry and couldn't eat. After supper, my brother Kerry and I were playing basketball and I tried to make an encouraging statement: "I'm sure

Dad and the crew all climbed into a dory with their life jackets on. They'll be okay." I didn't realize the severity of the storm conditions.

For the next week, life at school was quiet, like a funeral parlour. There were 385 students in our school and 73 children in our community were instantly left without fathers. Students and teachers didn't look us in the eye or speak to us. I guess they didn't know what to say. It was a long, lonely week.

Soon the official report came from the Canadian Navy base at Halifax. They had found my Dad's boat and sent divers to check out his cabin. Their report: "No Bodies Found". Because the boat was in such bad shape and a potential menace to other ships, they had to torpedo her and blow it up after two failed attempts at towing her to port. This meant that my mother couldn't sell what was left and she didn't get to keep any of the insurance money because it all went to the people who had just done a large over-haul of the boat during the winter months.

The headline from the newspaper, *The Halifax Chronicle*, read "The Storm That Broke Lockeport's Heart." Seventeen men died. Seventy-three children lost their dads in one night. The families of the surrounding community and the town of Lockeport, which had a population of twelve hundred, were shocked and devastated. Most of the people in this community were related. This tragedy affected everyone. I was absolutely numbed by it all.

The widows of Dad's four crew members arrived at our door one day after dark. There was so much hugging and crying that it took a long time for them to get through the door. Others were suffering just as much as my family. I did, however, overhear my mom say, "Arthur is the oldest boy and he understands. The other children don't." I remember thinking, "Me? I don't understand!"

The memorial service was held weeks later in the largest church in the town. Half of Lockeport came, over six hundred people. Only my mother and I attended from our family. The other children stayed home with a friend. What really struck me, while the names of the seventeen lost men were being read off, was that there were no bodies at the front, just lots of flowers. I had an empty feeling inside me and no real closure. I never heard the sermon that day because my mind was wandering. I got to thinking that, perhaps, Dad rowed to a nearby island, or maybe he got picked up by a freighter and taken to Africa or South America where he couldn't find a phone or anyone who spoke English. Years later, I would realize that this was just wishful thinking. I knew in my heart that the ocean was a mean, fearful, powerful place. I was well aware that hurricane-like storms, high winds and waves were deadly. And, with the wind chill factor well below zero, I knew deep down, Dad was lost— lost at sea.

After the service, the families made the long walk in the rain to the government wharf to put flowers into a boat to be taken out to sea. This ceremony is performed when sailors are lost at sea, because the ocean does not give up its dead. The bodies are gone forever. It was such a sad time.

Mom was hanging onto my arm and shaking so much she could hardly walk. She was so overcome with the emotion of it all. I had never felt so helpless as I did that day. Nanny, overcome with grief, said, "My boys just got up, walked out the door and never came back." She looked at me and gave me a long hug and cried for awhile and said, "You look just like your father."

A few months later, my brothers and I were helping Grampy pull his herring nets into the boat. A good friend, Vernon Murphy, steamed alongside and tried to bring sympathy to Grampy over the loss of his two boys. Grampy just shook his head and said, "My father was a volunteer preacher and made me go to Sunday School. This meant no playing baseball on Sundays. I said I would never force that on my boys. Now I regret that. You see, the men left at noon on Saturday and likely died Sunday or Monday. If I had raised them to go to church, they would have been there instead of at the bottom of the ocean. Now I have to teach Lawrence's six boys the ropes around a boat."

I was haunted by the thought that, on that fateful day, Dad likely remembered my last words to him. "Don't come back," I said, "until you catch forty thousand pounds of fish." Did he risk his life so that I would be proud of him? I wondered and worried some more: *"Did I cause my father's death?"* This thought would remain with me for a few months until one day Grampy made the statement: "Those boats were not made to go that far off shore at that time of the year."

With our only source of income gone, my mom had to let our full time housekeeper go. Dad had hired her to help Mom around the house. Many of the country folk helped as much as they could. One man gave my mom the money to send me to the Boy Scout World Jamboree in Quebec City and Ottawa. Don Messer and his Islanders put on a benefit concert and they raised seventeen hundred dollars for each of the widows. I overheard my mom say, "I don't care how poor we get. I'm not farming out my family. I'm keeping them together." This brought me much comfort.

Not all the people were kind, though. One day, a lady came to our house and bawled Mom out for not having a tombstone in Dad's memory. Mom was so shocked and stunned that she couldn't tell her it was on back order. She piled all seven children into the car and cried the whole way up to my Aunt Marjorie's house to find comfort. We almost ended up in the ditch because she was crying so hard. Another day a woman arrived at our home partially drunk and yelled at Mom, "If your husband hadn't gone fishing, my husband wouldn't have gone. Now I am left destitute with all these children." In other words, it was all my dad's fault and the blame would now have to fall on my mom. Mom just stood there in the doorway silent and hurting deeply. I felt like punching this lady, but Dad had taught me never to hit a woman under any circumstances.

Our family was in tatters, devastated and in pain beyond belief. My happy and fun-loving home was quickly becoming a faint memory. How would we cope? I had no answers. In my disillusionment, I was filled with questions, "What kind of loving God would allow this? Why didn't He take the town drunks and let my great father live?" Little did I know that, in time, God would soon provide answers to these questions in a remarkable way!

CHAPTER THREE

A Tom Sawyer's Life

My world had now been torn apart. As the years went by, I often reflected back on what a wonderful life I had before my dad was drowned. It was filled with laughter, fun and adventure—a 'Tom Sawyer' kind of life. The many activities I was involved in would be used of God later in my life to help me in His service, although at the time I didn't realize that.

My father, Lawrence Taylor, was from Little Harbour, Nova Scotia. Dad was drafted into the navy in 1943 and was sent to Prince Rupert, British Columbia for basic training. It was there he was trained how to fight the Japanese on a mine sweeper. He was taught how to capture the mines before they exploded and how to drop depth charges onto submarines. After the war, he stayed on the west coast and fished on a salmon boat. He also worked on a tug and barge but this work was hard on his back so he concentrated only on fishing.

My mother, Muriel Hughes, was from Burnaby, British Columbia. She attended Teachers' College for one year and then was assigned to teach English at a Japanese internment camp in Prince Rupert. It was in this town that she met my father and they were married by the Captain on board his ship. They settled in Vancouver where I was born. With my dad's decision to focus on fishing only, they decided to move back to Nova Scotia where my father had Bill Cox, a shipbuilder, make a 'long-liner' boat for him and resumed his fishing business.

Seven children eventually came along, with me being the eldest. Because of this, I was given many responsibilities. I had to collect the garbage and then dump it between the road and the ocean. I would either burn it or let the tide take it out. Sometimes the rats would eat it, but I would use my pellet gun or sling shot to rid our property of these pesky rodents. In the winter, I would split wood as well as carry coal to heat our home. I cut down balsam firs and sold them for Christmas trees, receiving ten, fifteen or twenty cents, depending on the size. In the spring, I would help repair our lobster traps and in the summer and fall, I would shear sheep, milk goats, cut hay with a scythe and pick berries— anything to make or save money for the family.

I got on very well with my brothers and sister. There was hardly any conflict. The same was true with my relationship with Mom and Dad. In fact, I can only remember being scolded twice by my parents. My father overheard me telling a dirty joke and he reprimanded me by saying that this was not a classy way to act. The other time, I rode my bike eleven miles to see a movie without telling Mom where I had gone. She was worried about me and told me to always tell her where I was going. There were only loving rebukes in the home.

My childhood was a typical, small village experience. We had no television or books to read in our home. The outdoor life is what excited me. Although I had no really close friends, I did have a few good acquaintances with whom I enjoyed other adventures. We would hike into the woods and look for rivers and ponds in which to catch trout. We would hunt rabbits, ducks, geese, and partridge to supply food for our families. We also attended Boy Scouts, where we learned how to cook, tie knots, do first-aid, and all about fire-safety procedures. I also learned many good character traits and how to have healthy relationships. These would all be very helpful in the future.

But being young and somewhat foolish, my adventures almost got me killed on a number of occasions. I could have drowned four times because of my fearlessness while on the water and nearly died from hypothermia while continuing to hunt after I got soaking wet on a cold Nova Scotia winter's day. Thanks to my friend, Gary Redding, I survived this episode. However, one incident put fear in me and made me realize that my life could be taken at any moment.

I was thirteen years old and on my way home with my friend, Allan Spidle, after our final baseball game of the season in October. There were many vacant properties in the area, many of them with apple orchards. It was common among some kids to steal a few apples and take them home to their mother so she could make them an apple pie. So, with this in mind, I went up one thick, leafy tree and Allan went up another. But on that day, a hunter happened to be driving by and thought he saw a deer eating an apple. Since the trees were just over a hill, only the top of the tree was visible to him. I was wearing a rabbit skin cap and had on a white shirt. He likely thought I was a white-tailed deer running away when my white sleeve appeared alongside my cap in the thick leaves. So he fired his rifle. The bullet came within a few inches of my head and the percussion was so loud it stunned me. I dropped out of the tree and screamed. The hunter took off, probably scared he had almost killed someone. I was not seriously hurt but this experience did put the fear of dying into me.

Another clear memory of my boyhood days was my early love of sports. I attended a one-room school in the country where children from kindergarten to Grade Five attended. Since school work didn't interest me, I found my passion in sports, especially baseball. I heard about 'stickball', but had never played it until a fellow classmate introduced the game to us when I was in Grade Five. He brought his dog's sponge ball from home and an old broomstick to hit the ball. Rocks were used as bases, which made it tough if you had to slide into a base. One time a friend hit a ball through a school window. He was so excited to get a home run, but not so thrilled when he got the strap for breaking the window. I did the same thing to my grandparent's home but I didn't receive a strapping. My dad had trained me to apologize and had taught me how to replace a broken window.

By the time I had reached Grade Seven, I was wearing a size fourteen shoe. Naturally, I became interested in the game of basketball. Orange crates bolted against the barn wall were used to attach the backboard and rim. We would have to dribble around rocks during a game. I wanted to improve my dribbling, so I rode my bike five miles to the nearest asphalt road to practice. I didn't make the school team that year, but I was determined to qualify in Grade Eight. To help achieve that, I cleared a site by cutting down some old trees. I placed them side by side on the ground for the foundation. One tree that had all the limbs removed became my pole to which the rim was then nailed. I then gathered some wooden planks that had washed up on shore from broken boats and made a platform on top of the tree foundation. I literally had a gym in my back woods. I practiced every time the weather was suitable and made the team the next year.

When I reached high school, sports had become my one true love. I had no desire to succeed academically at school. I had to repeat grades eight, ten and twelve. The only reason I stayed in school was to play sports. Shop class was the only exception. I was able to make shelves for my mom and baseball bats for our ball games. I even became interested in soccer. It was a rough sport because we were allowed to body check our opponents and kick mud on them. This was rather unsanitary because sewage from neighbouring homes drained into the field. However, I did have one memorable and glorious moment. With my size fourteen feet I once kicked a ball from in front of our goal into the other team's goal to win the game!

But my big feet also got me into some trouble. I remember one time being out trout fishing with a friend, Raymond Page, when my foot got caught in a beaver hole. People began to tease me about my big feet. It was said that all I needed was a set of oars and I could row across the back harbour on them. In my youth, I regretted having this clumsy 'handicap'. However, later in life when I had to jump five feet to land on a ship or else fall thirty feet into the water of the Welland Canal, I came to rely on those feet to save my life. Plus, I can also read Romans 10:15 with a smile: *"How beautiful are the **feet** of them that preach the gospel of peace, and bring glad tidings of good things!"*

As I got a little older, sports gave way to a new interest—I began to notice girls. Before I met Dorcas, I had dated six different girls and all of them broke up with me, breaking my heart in the process. It was easy to see why they didn't find me attractive. I had bad manners, poor grammar, I talked too fast, mispronounced words and did poorly academically. I also smelled. Our family had to share a well with another family so water was used sparingly. I only had one bath a week, usually Saturday night, and Mom would do a washing once a week as well. This meant that the clothes I wore to school gave off the odious smells of fish, bait and my sweat from playing sports. One girl even gave me a bottle of aftershave lotion to give me a subtle hint, but I thought it was girl's perfume so I didn't put it on.

In my last year of high school, I was elected president of the school's Student Council. I really didn't qualify with my poor language skills. My opponent, Tom Townsend, was a gifted speaker and went on to become a pastor, but I believe I won only because I was more popular and into sports. One good thing did come from my role as council president. I was forced to make speeches in front of people. Although I murdered the English language, it did help me get over my fear of speaking in front of crowds. This would prove to be beneficial when, later in life, I would have to preach before church congregations.

Despite my different adventures, my reflections always seem to come back to my dad. It was Dad who had taught me how to fish, hunt and get along with people. Now he was dead. But the impression he made on me would last a lifetime and the important values he taught me would shape my life in a big way.

CHAPTER FOUR

A Father's Love:
Gone but Not Forgotten

It was difficult to believe that our family had been left with such a big void to fill. As time passed, I began to appreciate the wonderful heritage that Dad and Mom had provided me. They set a wonderful example for me of love, kindness, patience, and an unselfish and caring attitude. Despite my mom's loss, she continued to demonstrate these qualities. For a long while, and even until this day, I think of the many times Dad thought of others instead of himself.

He certainly loved my mom. I never heard Dad ever raise his voice to Mom or say one negative thing to her, or about her to others. After every sword fishing trip, he would always bring her some chocolates or nylons or some other thoughtful gift. He would take her on three vacations a year: The Annapolis Valley Blossom Festival, the Lunnenburg Exhibition, and one deer hunting trip with some other couples. These may not seem like vacations today, but for a woman to go to a motel and a restaurant and have no household chores or family responsibilities was a big deal. In these ways my dad was a man 'ahead of his time'.

Dad showed a lot of sensitivity and wisdom in dealing with his children. He would set some rules for our wrestling games with him. We were not to push against the table leg for extra leverage because the table was on a level with the window sill. I got carried away one time and the table went right through the double-paned window. I was scared, knowing how other fathers and even Grampy would get upset and holler. However, Dad never raised his voice but just said that he needed a worker on Saturday to take the hooks off his fishing gear. It took me all day. We then went to Sutherland's Hardware Store and bought glass and all the needed materials to fix the window. He took the time to carefully show me all the tricks of sealing and putting the window in right. This would come in handy years later as I'd occasionally break windows around the Lockeport Ball Park during baseball games. I gladly repaired them and the windows that any of my teammates broke.

Dad treated his neighbours and fellow men with respect and fairness. One time, a neighbour named Roy Lloyd hit our car head-on at the top of Amos' Hill. He was on our side of the road so he was at fault. His meat truck bumper smashed in the grill of Dad's new car. I thought for sure my father would be upset, but he got out to see if Roy was okay, then said, "As long as the lights, hood and radiator are fine, you don't owe me a cent. I have no plans for trading in the car for a long time so what does it matter what the car looks like? As long as it gets me home to my dear wife, that's all I care about." They both had a laugh. Roy gave Dad a piece of meat from his delivery truck, and we were on our way. There was no calling the police or insurance company.

On another occasion, Dad and I went to pick up a crew member but he wasn't home. I watched something from the car I will never forget. The man's drunken wife asked Dad for a kiss but he refused.

She then slapped his face, cutting his lip. I loved my father so I yelled out the window and said, "Hit her, Dad, she hit you first!" What I saw changed my way of thinking forever. Dad gently took her arms and sat her down on a chair and she started to cry. He said something to make her laugh and then came back to the car. Of course I wanted to know why he didn't hit her. To this, Dad replied, "Real men don't hit women. Besides, she is drunk and I could lose her husband as a crew member and a friend. And my name would mean nothing if it got around town that I beat up a drunk woman." I decided right then and there that I was going to treat all women with respect.

My favourite recollections were the times my father and I would lie down on the couch together, his arm around me during his rest time, and we would both talk and listen – real communication. One on one with my best friend. It didn't get much better. Oh how I miss those precious moments.

In my opinion, Dad was everything a man should be. His sacrificial love to his family, friends and neighbours would influence me for the rest of my life. In fact, my hurt and emptiness was beginning to fade. What was happening to me? Was there really a God who cared about me? Could I really experience peace in the midst of my turbulent life? I was about to find out.

CHAPTER FIVE

Peace at Last!

Judy was very different from all the other girls I had known at school. She didn't go to dances or movies and she was very kind to me by helping me with my homework. I wondered, "Would she ever go out with a guy like me?" I finally built up enough courage to ask her on a date but her answer surprised me. She said, "I'll have to ask my father." I thought to myself, "I'm nineteen and she's eighteen. We're both adults! Why does she have to ask her dad?" But I said, "Okay."

I learned later that he was not too thrilled with me asking out his daughter. She was a true believer in the Lord Jesus and I wasn't. The Bible says that a child of God has nothing spiritually in common with an unbeliever and therefore they should not be together. However, Judy's father wanted to show me 'Christlike love' and set down some guidelines.

We were to double date, go to a restaurant and be home by 10:00 p.m. If I wanted to go on any other dates, I had to go to the Sunday evening 'gospel' meeting with her. I hated church. I found it boring and without purpose or meaning. "What does 'religion' have to do with dating? What does the word 'gospel' even mean?" I wondered. But I liked this girl so I said, "Okay. I will agree with these rules."

So on that Sunday, there I was listening to the preacher's message. He spoke on Romans 3:23, which says: *"For all have sinned and come short of the glory of God."* Over the next few weeks, I came under a deep conviction in my heart. What was this feeling I had inside? For a whole week, I had trouble sleeping. I wasn't paying attention in school. I had so much turmoil and distress within me. Later I would learn that God was drawing me to Himself.

I talked with Judy and said in self-defense, "Your minister said I was a sinner. He doesn't know me. I haven't robbed a bank or killed anybody. I am not a sinner!" She took her Bible out of her purse and turned to Romans 3:23 again. I asked if I could borrow her Bible to read this book of Romans.

In my reading of the book, I discovered that God ordains or permits governments to rule, even though they are not perfect. They make the laws by which the people are to live. We should obey these laws unless they go against God's Word, the Bible. Occasionally, I would break hunting, fishing and traffic laws. The simple conclusion: I was a sinner.

The next Sunday I attended church. I was still very uncomfortable, but I listened to the preacher carefully. He was preaching on a Bible verse from John 3:16, *"For God so loved the world that He gave his only begotten Son, that whosoever believeth in Him should not perish, but have everlasting life."* I wondered what in the world that meant. The only thing I knew about the Bible, prior to meeting Judy, was what I learned in Boy Scouts. There, I learned that someone named Noah brought animals two by two into a big boat. And at Christmas time, I heard something about a baby being born in a manger. As for Easter, it only meant chocolate eggs and bunnies to me.

After the meeting I approached the minister and said, "I am very troubled inside." He invited me to go into a back room to talk more about what I had heard. There the preacher told me to put my name into John 3:16. I repeated the verse, *"For God so loved **Arthur Taylor** that He gave His only begotten Son, that if **Arthur** believed in Jesus, **Arthur** would not perish, but **Arthur** would have everlasting life."* The preacher said that if I would pray to the Lord Jesus and believe that He died for my sins, and would ask Him to come into my life, He would forgive my sins and come in and take control of my life. I would receive eternal life with Jesus Christ and know for sure I would go to Heaven and not to Hell. He told me that this was the Gospel, the good news of Jesus Christ. At that point, I recalled hearing over the years that my dad was in Heaven and I loved him so much, I wanted to be with him too. I prayed a jumbled but simple prayer, thanking God for sending His Son, the Lord Jesus, to die for my sins personally. I asked Jesus to save me from my sins and to come into my life and be my Lord and Saviour. I could tell something happened. The guilt I had felt about wrong things I had done was gone! I felt a peace come over me. I knew I had eternal life. I was saved forever. God would remember my sins NO MORE!

I had the assurance in my heart that I would be in Heaven! God has said it in His word and I believed it. So on January 23, 1966, I was 'born again', that is, born spiritually into God's family.

When I came out of the back room, I found out that Judy and her friend, Janet, had been praying for me. Imagine, people would pray for me that I would put my faith in the Lord Jesus! It was overwhelming to me. I also realized that what had just taken place had given me a peace beyond all understanding.

One of the first thoughts that came to my mind as I left the church was, *"Why hadn't someone told me about this new life in Christ before? I had nearly died four times in the water and one time by a gun. If I had died, I would have gone to hell. Why hadn't some of my friends at school told me?"* They had lots of time because of the three grades I had to repeat!

I sensed an urgent need to get this good news out immediately to those that I knew. "What about all the fishermen going out to sea, putting their lives in danger just like my dad had done." Something was terribly wrong! Someone needed to tell them about Jesus. It was at that moment that the Lord took the reality of the tragedy of my dad's death at sea and gave me a burden for lost souls. I wanted to win them to Christ so they could have the assurance of knowing their sins would be forgiven and that they would have a home in Heaven. This burden has never left me, even to this day.

I returned to Judy's house where her father met me at the door. I told him I had just trusted in the Lord Jesus Christ as my personal Saviour. He said, "I know, I can see it in your face." I told my mom. She seemed pleased, but said nothing. I told my school friends and my fellow workers, as well as anyone I met, about my life-changing experience.

Starting the next week I went to church every time there was a meeting. Young People's, Sunday School, Prayer Meeting and both Sunday services. I couldn't get enough of being with fellow believers in Christ. Many of the Christians shared some advice to help me in my new walk and Robert Chymist gave me a Bible. In doing so, he put his finger over the word 'Holy'. He said, "This isn't just the Bible." He suddenly pulled away his finger and told me, "This is no ordinary book, it is the **Holy** Bible. It is everlasting and all powerful. God has inspired men to write His book. You should use it to guide you in every part of your life. His Word will give you wisdom." Others also encouraged me to read the Bible. Someone told me, "God's book is true. God has said it, that settles it, you believe it, now go and obey it."

I recall one Sunday sitting in the meeting when I became overwhelmed inside. I realized that my sins, as the Bible says, were as far away from God as the east is from the west. I was forgiven forever. I broke down and started to cry right in the middle of the preacher's message. My heart was filled with love and adoration for this Saviour of mine who suffered so much for me on the cross so that I could live eternally with Him in Heaven. My heart was filled with worship for the One who loved me and gave Himself for me.

Despite all the joy I had experienced over the last few weeks, there were some burning questions nagging inside me. What direction would my life take now? What would my family and friends think of me and my new life? How would they treat me? But a more pressing question pierced my mind, "Was my dad really in Heaven? Had he ever trusted in Christ?" I knew that only God knew for sure, but I had to find out.

CHAPTER SIX

Was Dad in Heaven?

Would I see Dad in Heaven? I began to ask people who knew my father. These were individuals who might be able to shed some light on my dad's spiritual background. I talked to Witman Swansburg who knew my dad since childhood. He reminded me that my Grampy's father was a part-time preacher. He had no formal education and wasn't qualified to do weddings. However, he preached the Bible at a house meeting for men, and at summer outdoor meetings. He also conducted Bible classes in the town and spoke at a local teen camp. Since he did public ministry, he was very strict with his children and required them to set a good example of what it was to be "spiritual" in those days. This meant that, on Sundays, you went to church, visited relatives, read, went for a walk, and sang songs. Mr. Swansburg told me that Dad did attend one of the Bible classes as a boy and received some teaching from God's Word. I'm sure this had some influence in laying the foundation for the way he approached life.

I talked to the widow of one of my dad's war buddies, Arthur Godfrey. She told me that her husband's and my father's warship docked in at British Columbia. While they were on leave, her husband took Dad to visit a Salvation Army centre. Here, two young and lonely sailors far away from home experienced some Christlike love and enjoyed the hymns played by their band. Back then, the Salvation Army not only stressed meeting the social needs of individuals but also the preaching of the Gospel and how to get to Heaven. They had a real concern for lost souls. Dad and his buddy listened to the simple message of Christianity presented there. Mrs. Godfrey was told by her husband that both he and my dad placed their faith in the Lord Jesus that night.

My search then led me to my best source yet, Mr. Errol Williams. He was one of my father's crew members but was not out to sea with them on that fateful trip. He hadn't been feeling well the day before and the doctor told him not to go. He told me of another time when the Muriel Eileen was caught in a bad storm off Sable Island. One crew member got down on his knees to pray in fear of death. Errol got inspired to share the good news gospel of Christ with the men. Dad said to him later, "I believe in that message the way you explained it." This was great news!

Looking back on my home life, I can now see evidence in my dad and his life of many Christlike qualities. His love and kindness to family, friends and acquaintances tell me of an inner belief in the Lord. While God alone knows for sure, I am confident that my dad was a believer in the Lord Jesus Christ and, therefore, in Heaven.

Having come to grips with my dad's spiritual condition and enjoying the peace that I would likely see him again in Heaven one day, I then turned my attention to those who still needed to hear the good news of Jesus Christ.

However, before I was to experience much of the joy of sharing my testimony with others, I would hear my aunt, a nurse, say to my mom,"The doctor says that Arthur may not live through the night!"

CHAPTER SEVEN

Near-Death and Discouragement

M y health problem started one day when I began getting severe pains in my side. I thought nothing of it, "Probably just a pulled muscle," I figured. The pain increased in intensity so I went to see our local doctor. He determined it was my appendix. I was told I had to get to a hospital immediately. However, the nearest hospital was seventy-five miles away and I had no way to get there. A neighbour, Hobert Pearce, volunteered to take me in his rickety old truck to the hospital. During the trip, I sensed a sudden relief from the severe pain so we took our time. We stopped to look at ducks and a moose for awhile along the way.

After a two hour ride, we eventually arrived at the hospital. I informed the admitting nurse that my pain had eased an hour and a half earlier and that I didn't think I needed an operation. However, I learned that this was an indication that my appendix had already ruptured. Unfortunately, the doctor on-call was not aware that this amount of time had passed and that the matter from my appendix had already started to spread throughout my abdomen. Therfore, he didn't insert the customary tubes into the incision to drain any residue infection from my abdomen. Instead, he said, "This boy is big and strong. We'll just give him double penicillin and he will be fine." Within a very short time though, I got Peritonitis and went into a coma.

When you are in a coma, you can't see, talk or move—but you can hear. I heard my aunt tell my mom two nights in a row, "The doctor says that Arthur may not live through the night; He is a very sick boy." By all accounts I should have died. I thought, "I don't want to die. I don't believe my family is saved. I need to share the Gospel. Lord, please help me." I didn't fear death, but I wanted to live so I could share my faith with them.

God heard my prayer and in His mercy and according to His sovereign will, He spared my life. Why? Perhaps it was a message to my mom, aunt and the medical staff, that there is a God and He can perform miracles in this day and age. But this I knew for sure, that God wanted to use me to tell others the Gospel, the good news about how they could have their sins forgiven.

My life had been spared—again. Now I was even more determined to share my new found faith in the Lord Jesus with my family, friends and fish plant workers. They were beginning to see that this new life was real. The Lord gave me victory over swearing and telling off-coloured jokes. They were starting to see that God can change a life. So I tried not to miss a single opportunity. I put a Gospel tract in every student's desk at my high school but my homeroom teacher reported me to the principal. I was called into his office and he told me that I could not hand out 'religious' material in a public school. I said, "I didn't know that." I told him, "I wanted people to hear the Gospel before they died so that they could go to Heaven and not Hell." The principal would later tell my teacher that I was just going through a phase. This was no phase. My new life in Christ was forever.

While my zeal and boldness both were evident, my message was somewhat confusing. I would misquote verses, present sin, Christ and Heaven in such a confusing way it was difficult for people to understand what I was saying. I really didn't feel I was explaining it very well.

The local church I attended was surprised at my boldness. In those days, many Christians kept their faith within the four walls of the church building. Some leaders of the church thought that if you went into someone's fish house, you might hear swear words, see filthy pictures, or even be influenced to smoke or drink. No, the proper procedure was to advertise a meeting, invite people to come to church or call them on the phone. "Arthur," they said, "you are going to make the church look bad. You are getting some things backwards and you don't know the Bible that well." Their advice to me was to either stop talking to people about God unless it was at church, or to go somewhere and learn the Bible since the minister had left town.

This indeed was a crisis situation and caused me some anxiety as my heart wanted to see fishermen get 'saved' before they might lose their life at sea.

But my mind was rather confused with my lack of spiritual knowledge. However, they were older and, I assumed, much wiser. So my reaction was, "Well, I guess they know what they are talking about." So I prayed to God and asked Him to help me learn the whole Bible, verse by verse, so I could tell others about it. I had a real peace in my heart that God would answer my prayer. The new dilemma before me, though, would be an offer of $21,000 to go to university. Which one should I choose? Bible School or university?

CHAPTER EIGHT

God's Atheist

One of my high school teachers, Carl Palmer, was a religious man who was growing very concerned about my life and education. He offered to pay for all my expenses at Dalhousie University in Halifax. He wanted me to take the seven-year Teacher's College program at a cost of three thousand dollars a year. Upon completion of this course, I would have a teaching degree in Physical Education. It had been my dream since I was thirteen to teach 'gym'. But, I had made a promise to God to learn His Word so I could preach the Gospel. I had read in the Bible that we are to give ourselves completely to the Lord which is our reasonable service (Romans 12:1). So I thought to myself, "Arthur, just forget about the $21,000 and put God first." I was committed to following the Lord wherever He would lead me.

I was convinced that the only way I was going to learn more about the Bible was to go to a Bible School and this was exactly where the Lord led me. I applied to a number of schools and was rejected by each one. I did not qualify academically. I had only passed high school because I think some of the teachers liked me or felt sorry for me because of our family tragedy. In fact, I had been passed on trial for grades eight and nine English, but had failed it in grades ten through twelve—not the best subject to do poorly in if you wanted to teach the Bible.

I was told I might be able to get into a Bible School in Chicago if I wrote a special entrance exam in Toronto. But I couldn't afford the cost of the exam or the travel expenses from Nova Scotia. Even my mom didn't think it was a good idea. She told me, "They don't pay preachers very much." I was disappointed. Nobody wanted me, or so I thought.

Pryor Stewart, a Christian teacher in my high school, offered to write Moody Bible Institute in Chicago, Illinois on my behalf. His message to them was: "Arthur is a diamond in the rough. You should seriously consider accepting him." He also included a statement from Vic Williams: "God has His hand upon Arthur in a special way." The school wrote back to me and asked, "Why do you want to come to our school? Why do you think God is leading you here?" My answer was simple: "People are dying in my town every year and most of them don't know Jesus Christ personally. They are going to hell and don't know it. I don't know enough about the Bible. I want to come and learn God's Word in order to help these people." I would later learn that the Admissions Board, when they received my letter, said, "How can we refuse this guy? Our school's founder, D.L. Moody, wanted to teach people the Bible and get them out of the pews and into the street and put the 'Go' into the Gospel." They sent me an official form stating I had been accepted to the fall session at Moody Bible Institute in Chicago. However, I would have to take the 101 English course in the first year. Two important questions needed to be answered. First, how was I to pay for my schooling? And, second, where exactly was Chicago?

I would need one thousand dollars for the first year of school. Even though the tuition was free,

I had to pay for such things as room and board, health insurance, student activity fees, an airplane ticket and cab fare to get to the school.

My mom was still against me going. She reminded me that there were no degrees in Bible School. She didn't have the money. Neither did the rest of my family and friends. They did not see the need to learn of Christ, so why would they help me? There were no local church groups that would sponsor me because I didn't belong to any official missionary organization. Where was I to get the money?

Thanks to Arch Peterson, who supervised the local fish plant, I managed to get a job there. I thought I would work for the next eight months, earn enough money to go to school in Chicago and hope to learn more about the Bible. It seemed to be such a perfect plan. However, because of an extended recovery after my near death experience with my appendix and coma, I was unable to finish working for the last two months. Now where would I get the rest of the money?

But God had already set the answer in motion a while back. The short time that I had worked at the fish plant, I received a great deal of persecution over my faith in Christ from Eric Bennam, a self-professing atheist. He would tease me, call me names and make fun of the Bible. However, God's Word says that we are to have love for one another. Since it was extremely cold in the freezer part of the fish plant, I gave him my homemade mittens, socks and sweaters which my mom had made for me. He received these gifts with deep appreciation. I am sure he wondered why I, the young man whom he had been giving such a hard time, would show such kindness. I was just following our Lord's command to "love those who persecute you." My actions towards him affected him in a remarkable way.

When Eric heard about my sickness and that I wouldn't be able to go to Bible School, he decided to take a hat around the plant and collect money for me. Imagine an atheist collecting money for me to go and learn more about God! Little did he know that he, himself, was doing God's work. How marvelous are His ways!

This man collected one dollar from just about everybody at the plant which totalled two hundred dollars! Considering the people only made eighty cents to a dollar an hour, this was quite an offering. I now had exactly enough money for my first year of Bible School.

Preparing to leave Lockeport, I was filled with mixed emotions. I was sad to leave the place that had been home to me all my life. My girlfriend, Judy, and I had already parted ways when I started talking about going away to study the Bible. She was moving to Halifax and I was heading off to Bible School. A long distance romance just would not work. My heart was breaking. I loved my family and friends, the outdoor life, sports and sharing my faith. Yet, I grew more and more excited to see what God had planned for my future. I believed that God had called me and was leading me, and I believe He gave me the grace to say "good-bye" to my beloved hometown. The song "Farewell to Nova Scotia" comes to mind.

So off I went to Chicago. Sure, it was bigger than anything I had experienced, not to mention in a different country but, after all, people are people no matter where you go. I assumed life would be pretty much the same, just different scenery. Was I ever in for a shock, one that would nearly cost me my life.

CHAPTER NINE

Crocodile Dundee, Chicago Style

It was 1967 and I was twenty-one years old. I had just embarked on a lifelong journey that would hopefully make me an effective witness for Christ. How exciting! What could possibly go wrong? Plenty.

I landed in Toronto on my way to Chicago, only to find the plane I was to take had broken down and wouldn't be available until the next day. So here I was, stuck in a big city with no money for a motel. What else could I do but walk along the highway to find downtown Toronto, my suitcase in one hand

and my broken-handled duffel bag tucked under my other arm. Apparently, this was not a common practice in Toronto. In fact, I found out later that it was illegal to hitch-hike on busy highways, but I didn't know that then.

After asking several people if they could point me to a church that might be open, I found one with the minister working inside. He offered me a place to sleep for the night in the church manse. He asked me my motivation for going to Bible School. I told him how I was saved and that I wanted to preach God's saving message to everybody. His response was, "You sound like Billy Graham." He believed one's faith was a private matter and shouldn't be talked about. Even though I disagreed with him, I was very appreciative of his kind hospitality. The next day he took me back to the airport.

When I landed at O'Hare Airport in Chicago, I had to go through something called "Customs", which I had never heard of before. The agent said, "Where is your passport?" I replied, "What is a passport?" I told him I was going to go to school at Moody. He said, "Where is your paper from the school to say you are accepted?" My answer was, "I didn't know

I needed to bring that." Things were going from bad to worse rather quickly.

Out of desperation, he finally said, "I see you have a Bible there. I believe you and I'll let you into the country but you must report to the immigration office downtown with the school's form as soon as you get there." That's the sovereignty of God!

I grabbed a cab to take to the school. I had never been in a taxi cab before. I had budgeted three dollars for the ride to the school. When the driver hit his meter it was one dollar before we even started. We had gone only a short distance on the expressway when the meter hit three dollars. I said, "Let me out at this exit." The shocked driver said, "This is a bad neighbourhood. It's very dangerous." I smiled and said, "That's all right. I get along with everybody. Where I come from we have French, Blacks, Native Canadians and even Germans. We all love one another and try to help each other. I'll just 'thumb' my way to the school." The driver just shook his head and said, "You'll get robbed or even killed in this area."

As I opened my bag to pay him, he saw my student handbook and a picture of the entrance arch to Crowel Hall, the administrative building, on the cover. He looked at me and said, "I know where that is. I'll take you there, no charge!" This was another example of the hand of God clearly at work.

I had a meeting with my Dean of Students, Robert Irvin. After hearing my whole story of all the events that took place to get me to the school, his comment was: "It certainly is God's will that you are here." He reissued me the form I needed and told me to go downtown to immigration and get my situation sorted out. As I left the school, I saw two lines of cars stopped at something called a 'stop light' while the people crossed the street. I thought, "How nice! Everyone here stops for the walkers!" Now I had never crossed a street using stop lights before. We only had stop signs back home in Lockeport.

When I got to the light, I didn't realize it had turned red so I kept on walking across the four-lane street. The cars started moving across the intersection as I tried to get to the other side. The horns blaring, I just kept making my way across the street thinking to myself, "Isn't this nice— being friendly to an out-of-towner!" Back home, we always honked and waved greetings to one another. But when I had to start dodging cars to the other side of the street, I suddenly realized what was really happening. It's a miracle I made it across at all!

Friends would later tell me that I reminded them of a man called Crocodile Dundee, a fictional character who left his native Australian Outback and was met with a major culture shock when living in New York City. This pretty well described most of my initial experiences in Chicago. I was learning that, contrary to what I had thought just a few days before, life was going to be different here, very different.

CHAPTER TEN

Lots to Learn

P art of our education was to go out into the city and show Christlike love to all. I became involved in teaching a Sunday School class of forty-three boys, ten years of age. We were to meet in a Day Care building for eight months; I had a desire that the Lord would save at least one soul for each month I was there.

I soon learned that I had a real challenge before me. I had little control over this class which soon began to resemble a zoo. On my birthday, they thought it would be fun to honour me with a spanking. They got books, broomsticks, paddles, and anything else that could possibly inflict pain. Trying to be gracious, I let them spank me twenty-two times. This activity caused Mr. Tahl, the head of the Christian Work Department to shake his head and say: "You need prayer." Well, despite my missteps, I survived that eight-month assignment "by the seat of my pants." The best part was that God, in His grace, saved eight boys on my last day with them! My prayer had been answered and my desire for eight boys' salvation had been fulfilled!

On other occasions, I would go into tough neighbourhoods to share my testimony with Open Air Campaigners, an organization that had a bus with a pull down platform on the side. We would run across drug addicts, alcoholics, hippies and gangs. I was sworn at, made fun of, and had bottles thrown at me. Believe it or not, I had very little fear. I knew the Lord was leading and guiding me and these folks needed to be shown love and to hear of Jesus' sacrificial love for them. They were lost and needed Christ desperately.

I believed I should try and be friendly to everyone I met. Walking down the city streets I would say, "Good Morning" to everybody, only to receive strange looks. One day I got lost in downtown Chicago. I walked up to a little old lady, about five feet tall, to ask for help. I tapped her on the shoulder from behind and she screamed and ran away. I found out later why she was scared. Apparently this was the method thieves used to rob women. They would work in pairs. One would tap you on the shoulder and the other would grab your purse and run.

My awkward moments carried over into my public speaking experiences. Preaching was not my strong point. I spoke too fast, used broken sentences, and my grammar was terrible. On one occasion I signed up to go to the Chicago Rescue Mission with a fellow student who was a gifted speaker. I was there to observe and hopefully learn something.

On the way to the mission, the preacher got very sick, and I was asked to take his place. So I took about ten minutes and put together a little sermon on John 3:16. We had three girls with us who sang in a trio and then sat down behind me on the platform. I started to give my first sermon in my life and I was feeling awful. All of a sudden two men, who turned out to be drunk, got up from the audience and started down the aisle. I thought, "Wow! They're already coming forward to put their faith in Christ and I haven't even given the invitation yet!"

Then I heard one of them growl, "She's mine!" The other yelled back, "No, she's mine!" I realized they were fighting over the girls behind me. The director of the mission broke up the fight and moved the girls to the back row. I was so befuddled that I couldn't even quote John 3:16. I was finished. I had to sit down. The director finished my sermon. I had failed totally, but God hadn't!

I had invited a man off the street to come to the meeting. He stayed behind. We had a long talk and he trusted Christ as his Saviour. The Lord humbled me that night, but He did show me that my ministry was better with one-on-one.

After returning to the school, I reflected on all that had happened. I thanked God for saving a lost soul. But I also began to think, "What a strange thing for those guys to be thinking of girls from a Bible School— and right in the middle of a message!" And yet, for some reason, it didn't seem so strange when I began to do the same thing.

CHAPTER ELEVEN

The Art of Love

I enjoyed my time at Bible School. I lived in a dormitory and shared a floor with eight other men. We had great times together studying the Bible, laughing, playing basketball and having Friday night water fights with Ron Phillips and Jerry Jenkins.

As in the past, it was the academic side of school that proved to be a struggle for me. During the Old Testament Survey course, our teacher began a brief talk about the life of Gideon. He assumed everyone in the class knew about this man, since he thought everyone would have, at the very least, a basic knowledge of the Bible. Everyone did, except me. Since the course was running a little behind schedule he was going to skip the story of this judge of Israel. I put my hand up and asked, "Who is Gideon?" He kindly explained the story to me and throughout the rest of the course he took his time presenting the material, knowing my limited Bible knowledge.

Research papers were new to me. We were never required to do them in high school. I didn't have a clue what a bibliography or footnotes were. My writing skills were poor, filled with spelling mistakes, incomplete sentences and 'made up grammar'. My marks were generally in the C to C- range at best. That would all change soon, not by an improvement in my skills, but through a trip to the school's infirmary.

At the beginning of this same school term, a young lady by the name of Dorcas Frey had been hired by the school to be the assistant head nurse in the infirmary. Dorcas had just graduated from Emmaus Bible School in Oak Park, a suburb of Chicago, and was looking forward to serving the Lord by caring for people.

As a result of my extended recovery from my burst appendix and peritonitis, I had developed a cyst on my tailbone. It had bothered me for some time. The cyst suddenly became infected and had become an open draining wound. This serious problem forced me to have an operation at the local hospital to remove the pilonidal cyst. Three weeks of my recovery was to be spent in the care of the school's infirmary. When I was transferred to this facility, the nurse on duty was none other than Dorcas Frey.

During the second week of my stay, a fellow patient in the infirmary said to me, "You and Dorcas have a lot in common. You both love the Lord and are from Canada. The two of you love sports, you're both outgoing and care about people. Besides, I can tell that she likes you. You should ask her out on a date." My response was, "No, I don't think so. She is a little older, more sophisticated, and better educated than me and she's my nurse! I heard that students don't date employees." My friend persisted in challenging me to date her so I finally, and very cautiously, approached her with the subject.

My "wife-to-be" recalls our meeting from a different perspective. She would later tell people:

"The day that I brought Arthur home from the hospital and admitted him to our nine-bed inpatient health care unit will be forever etched in my memory. It was during semester

break in January of 1968. Most of the students had gone home for the break, so there was little activity in our health service that day. Since I was the nurse on duty for the remainder of the day, and no one was around who needed my services, Arthur and I spent the whole time finding out about each other's life stories and backgrounds. He told me all about Judy, the girl who was instrumental in bringing him to salvation, and how they dated for about a year and a half. He showed me her picture and told me how sad he was when she decided to break up with him. She did not want to be away from Arthur for the three years while he was at Bible School. I tried to encourage him to keep in touch with her and that she might just change her mind some day.

Arthur wanted to know if there was anyone whom I was dating. I told him I had a few dates with one student but I didn't think anything would develop from it. I then shared with him how the Lord had made me content to remain single. This issue had been a real struggle for me. One time I would tell the Lord I was content, but then soon would start thinking that, because I was content, the Lord would reward me and bring someone along. Finally, I prayed and asked the Lord if my lot was to be single, would He please make me content and also fill my life with something else. He did; it was my job at Moody Bible Institute. I realized that this was the 'something else'.

Arthur maintained that I shouldn't give up and that the Lord might still have a life partner for me. My response was that if He did have someone for me, that would be great. But in the meantime, I was happy. Nevertheless, Arthur was going to pray for me because he thought the Lord had someone right around the corner for me. With that statement, he went around the corner to go back to his room since it was time for me to go off duty. Arthur will be quick to assure you that he did not think it would be him. He did not think of me in that way. But I was definitely impressed with him and it wasn't long before our 'chats' turned into something a little more serious."

Dorcas and I would go for long walks in the parks or botanical gardens. It was important to us to be 'public' in our dating and not allow ourselves to be found in compromising situations that could hurt our testimony as Christians. We became good friends and we found it very easy to talk with each other. The next step in our relationship, we believed, was to worship together. I decided to leave the place where I was attending. The church had over three thousand people and I only got to know a few of them. So Dorcas and I went to Woodside Bible Chapel. They had about one hundred and thirty people. It had a family atmosphere that made us feel welcome instantly. The personal fellowship was marvelous.

I had never heard of a "New Testament assembly" before, which Woodside was. I loved the way they worshipped the Lord Jesus Christ and observed the Lord's Supper every Sunday. The Lord Jesus had the preeminence in this group of believing Christians. They sought to follow the pattern of meeting together the way God had designed it in the New Testament. They were non-denominational and accountable to no 'headquarters' but simply to the Lord. They were an autonomous group of believers.

I had been accustomed to topical preaching, but at Woodside I was introduced to expository preaching, listening to such outstanding Bible scholars as Robert J. Little, Dan Smith, and John Phillips. I learned more from these preachers in some areas than I had at Bible School. Dorcas and I put all our efforts into serving the Lord at Woodside, getting involved in as many outreach programs as possible.

So Dorcas says she met a handsome, outgoing young student who was on fire for God who came under her care in the infirmary for three weeks. She would later say that she was "attracted to the spirituality and the zeal of this young man." As for me, I had the added bonus of my grades going up to B's and even A's because of my private tutor. Dorcas and I were married June 7, 1969 at the end of my second year and our first son, Mark Andrew, was born two years later while I was still studying at Moody.

Married life was not always a bed of roses. I had to pay my many bills at school and had to provide for my wife and son. To help make ends meet, we moved into Lydia Children's Home, a Christian place for children from broken homes. Here we were the house parents for ten teenage boys. Dorcas also took on the position of being the nurse for the home. It was a difficult, but interesting time, and the Lord helped us through it. My time at Moody was soon coming to an end. But then what? I now had a family to look after, but had no idea what was around the corner.

CHAPTER TWELVE

A Call to the Canal

I still had a burning desire to return to Lockeport and preach God's Word to lost sailors and their families. Yet, I was troubled by my lack of biblical knowledge even though I had studied three years at this school. I approached Mr. Robert Irvin, my personal dean, and expressed my concern. I told him, "While I've been here, I've had to study Christian music, mission work, Christian education and public speaking, but I have not studied every book of the Bible verse-by-verse. Would it be possible for me to stay for a fourth year and focus my studies on the books of the Bible that I missed during my three-year Pastoral Course?" After checking with the proper authorities, his answer came back as a "Yes" and so I became Moody's first post-graduate student. Little did I know then just how important this extra year at Moody would be in God's plan for my life. Meanwhile, events were occurring that would not change my desire to serve the Lord, but would certainly change the location where I would ultimately serve Him.

In St. Catharines, Ontario, Pastor Cameron Orr had been diagnosed with terminal cancer. He was the chaplain of the Welland Canal Mission. He had a desire, no doubt from the Lord, to find someone to take his place as chaplain to the sailors. He traveled to several Bible Schools looking for such an individual but had no success.

By now, I was nearing the end of my extra year of Bible study at Moody. Mr. Orr decided to make a telephone call to Dean Irvin whom he knew personally from the days when Mr. Irvin was ministering in Sarnia, Ontario. He asked him, "Would it be worth my time and effort to come to Moody to talk to the students about serving the Lord on the Welland Canal?" Robert wracked his brain to think of someone at the school who might be a good candidate. At that very moment, I walked into the Dean's office to get his signature on some official papers. I heard, "Just a minute, I have a Nova Scotia fisherman here who might be interested." He gave me a brief explanation of the work and asked me if I would be willing to meet with Mr. Orr. I agreed to this, so arrangements were made to have him come and speak to the student body.

At about the same time, I received a letter from a fishing friend back home in Nova Scotia. He told me how many of the fishermen for whom I had a burden, were having difficulty making a living in the area. Some of them were packing up their families and moving up to the Great Lakes region in Ontario because of more job opportunities in the shipping industry. I started to think that maybe God wanted me, not in my hometown, but at the Welland Canal Mission in St. Catharines, Ontario.

Mr. Orr came to the school and made a presentation about the canal ministry to the entire student body. He told us of the persecution from some sailors, captains and, at times, from the canal workers, even though most of them were respectful and thankful for our presence on board. He also shared how he sometimes got sick from eating foreign food while riding the ships. He bluntly explained the danger in jumping on and off the ships, especially during bad weather. We would face much of the world's religions, cultures and languages. However, if we were "wise as serpents and harmless as doves," God would provide the greatest opportunities to preach the gospel on ships from all over the world. You are literally a 'foreign missionary in the home port'. He appeared to have scared everybody. All five hundred male students left, except me. I had a previous arrangement to have lunch with him and I was definitely interested.

During our lunch, Mr. Orr made it clear he was not interested in my marks, but my burden for lost souls. He knew about my background, the death of my dad, and a desire to share God's free gift of salvation with sailors. He was aware that I knew the lingo of a sailor such as port, starboard, galley and bridge. He had heard about my boldness and my love towards people. Still, I wondered if I was qualified. He said to me, "Arthur, God doesn't call the qualified, He qualifies the called." But I was still lacking confidence in my abilities and felt the need for more training in the Bible and in counseling. After all, I was only twenty-five years old and still a relatively new Christian.

He agreed with me that I should take one more year and, this time, it was in Toronto, Ontario at what was then Ontario Bible College (OBC). To finance this year, we moved in with a widower and his two sons, ages four and six. Dorcas would be the housekeeper/cook/babysitter-nanny for all six of us (our son, Mark, was nine months old). It was a challenge for her at times but the Lord gave her strength as needed.

After my meeting with Mr. Orr at Moody, he returned to St. Catharines and met with the mission board. He told them that he had checked my background and found out I was the son of a ship's captain. At Bible school I had helped in the prison ministry, the rescue mission and preached in open air meetings. He told the mission board, "I have found God's man for the work as chaplain on the Welland Canal."

He told everybody of his conviction—except me. It wasn't until later while I was visiting churches all over Southern Ontario that I found out that he had been telling everyone that, the next year, Arthur Taylor would be there in his place. He had been doing this for about seven months already before I even felt peace from the Lord that this is where He wanted me to serve Him. After I confirmed with Mr. Orr that I would succeed him, he made arrangements for me to come to St. Catharines to meet with the board of directors.

Don Ralph, a fellow student at OBC, encouraged me about this ministry, stating that he knew of it and that it was a great work. He said I would probably need a resume and references. These words were not even in my vocabulary.

I didn't need to fear. As I entered the room (expecting a long and intensive interview), the board chairman, Skip Gillham, said, "Cameron tells us that you are God's man to follow him, so you are accepted." Another board member, Frank Ewald, added, "The torch has been passed." David Rennicks, also a board member, then explained that the Welland Canal Mission was a faith mission and that Cameron Orr had faith that God had called me to this work, which was good enough for them.

Mr. Orr had planned to train me, but he died just days before I was to start on July 1, 1972. There would be no training for me. The board members had only a limited knowledge of the work on a ship so I was somewhat left on my own. As it turned out, the lack of training probably was a good thing. As Mrs. Orr said to me, "If my husband had trained you, he would have tried to mold you into what he was like." Instead, God allowed me to use my talents and spiritual gifts to develop my own approach with sailors.

It is interesting to note here that the Lord had given Dorcas peace about this new sphere of service at the very time I first mentioned my meeting with Cameron Orr that day in Chicago. She didn't tell me this until I shared with her that I had received peace about it myself. The Lord graciously called us each separately to serve Him together.

And so in 1972, I became the fourth Welland Canal Chaplain in the one-hundred-and-four years of this ministry. But the difficult times that Cameron Orr warned me about were quickly heading my way.

CHAPTER THIRTEEN

Me and My Two Left Feet

I was soon thrust into a life filled with activity. My immediate task was to talk with the St. Lawrence Seaway Authority in order to establish, and hopefully maintain, a good working relationship. To this day, the Lord has helped me to do this.

I then began handing out New Testaments, gospel tracts, hand-played card talks, tapes, booklets, and, later on, videos to sailors on the ships. I would sometimes be laughed at, mocked, scorned, and some people would even swear at me. On one occasion, a sailor punched me in the chest and knocked me flying after I told him that God said he was a lost sinner. I just stood up, said that I forgave him like God has forgiven me, and continued handing out my literature. The Bible tells us we are to turn the other cheek and so I did, even though the back of my head was quite sore from hitting the steel bulkhead. I knew that wherever there is a work for the Lord, there would be persecution. My job was to show them Christlike love and trust Him for wisdom and the right things to say and do.

This ministry was a learning process for me and I learned a big lesson in my first year in what I said to sailors. I would walk up to someone on the ship and say, "Are you a Christian? Do you believe in Jesus Christ?" If they said yes, I'd say, "Oh wonderful! That means you're going to Heaven!" After about two years of visiting these men and seeing no growth in their Christian walk, I started asking more questions and I found out most weren't believers after all. They believed about Christ in their head, but they were not 'saved' and I had given them false assurance. So I tried to figure out all the ships that I had been on and looked for the men that I had talked with and tried to straighten it out. Some of the men did place their faith in the Lord Jesus, but I never knew for sure whether or not I revisited everyone I had met during my first years. Were there still men thinking they were going to Heaven because 'Chaplain Taylor' told them so? That was a bad mistake.

Something else I had to be extremely careful about was to identify the nationality of the person with whom I was talking. There are thirty-seven countries and fifty-five languages represented by the ships that travel the canal. Not all nationalities get along with one another. I found this out the hard way. One day, I went up to a cook on a ship and asked him if he was Chinese. He wasn't! He was Japanese and he chased me out of the galley, waving a meat cleaver at me.

On another occasion, I met a forty-year-old female sailor on a ship from France. Her husband had died and she had twin boys back home whom she missed very much. Through an interpreter, I was able to communicate that I couldn't do anything to over-come her loneliness, but I would be glad to mail her letters to her boys.

On the ship's return trip from Thunder Bay, Ontario, I met her again on the canal. My interpreter was not available but I had my trusty French-English dictionary. I attempted to ask her, "How are your twins?" However, the word for twins and legs are almost the same. So here was a twenty-six-year-old man asking a forty-year-old lady, "How are your legs?" She gave me a disgusted look and said, "Fermez la bouche." I knew what that meant, "Shut your mouth." She told the rest of the ship's crew, "The preacher insulted me. Don't have anything to do with him or take his literature." Later on, a French captain taught me how to apologize to her in French. She forgave me, but I learned that I must be very careful with the words I use.

Yet, all of these embarrassing situations (and many others) were helping to shape me for the work that God had "Taylor-made" for me. I soon found out that there was a tremendous need for counselling among sailors. So I offered to perform free wedding ceremonies and marriage counselling both before and after a couple was married. This opened up a number of opportunities to share the Gospel. I would only marry a couple who were either both believers in the Lord Jesus or who were both unbelievers. The Bible makes it clear that a believer and an unbeliever should not marry. There were other cases when I felt

Above: The happy newlyweds, Lawrence and Muriel.

Left: As a young sailor, Lawrence, in his navy cadet uniform in Halifax.

Lawrence and Muriel were married on board the navy ship by the ship's captain (on the left). Best man is Arthur Godfrey, after whom I was named.

Above: My father Lawrence, all ready to go hunting. I grew very close to him through hunting experiences.

Left: Grampy Taylor with a prize Canada goose he brought home to help feed the family. I received many good tips from him on how to bring home "the big one".

Our five-bedroom home by the ocean at the end of the Point in East Ragged Island. I spent most of my childhood and teenage years in this home.

Above: The fifty-three foot fishing long-liner MURIEL EILEEN that Lawrence had for his fishing career when he returned to Nova Scotia from BC. She was named after his wife and her sister.

Left: Lawrence (on left) and his brother, Mitchell, who were both lost in the storm. Each was the captain of his own fishing boat.

Arthur, Kerry, Ken, & John displaying some of the sweaters that their mother, Muriel, knitted for them each year from the wool of their sheep.

Below: The last Christmas that our happy family had together. Lawrence was lost at sea in March. I am in the centre at the back holding a hunting gun.

Above: The seven children now fatherless, and as the eldest I had to take on more responsibility. From left, back row - John, Ken, Kerry, myself. Front row - Gordon, George, and Heather.

Left: Myself as the young man who required post-operative care in the infirmary where I met Dorcas for the first time at Moody Bible Institute in Chicago.

Above: The sanctuary of the church building in which I first heard the gospel. A few weeks later I was led into the little side room where I confessed that I was a lost sinner and invited Jesus Christ to be my personal Saviour. The burdens of my soul were lifted! *Inset:* A few years ago we were reconnected with Brother Eustace Marshall and his wife. He was the preacher who led me to the Lord that night.

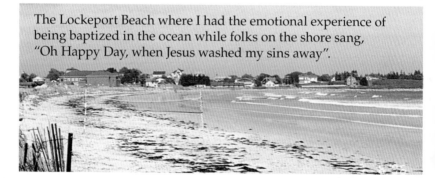

The Lockeport Beach where I had the emotional experience of being baptized in the ocean while folks on the shore sang, "Oh Happy Day, when Jesus washed my sins away".

The Lockeport Fish Plant where about 200 fellow workers took up a collection to help me go to Bible School.

Above left: Graduation Day.
A highlight of my education at
Moody Bible Institute (MBI) were the
experiences I had while doing my
practical Christian work assignments,
which included visitations at the jail
and the rescue mission.

Above right: Special dates began
with the Jr/Sr Banquet at MBI and I
have followed my dad's example of
"dating" my wife Dorcas frequently
ever since.

Left: Just above the bus in this photo
is the familiar sight of the arches
that the taxi driver recognized on
the cover of my student handbook
and then gave me the rest of the
ride free of charge.

Above: Our wedding day, June 7, 1969 at Wallenstein Bible Chapel.
Left to right: Heather (my sister), Sharon Frey (Dorcas' sister-in-law),
Marlene Toye and Esther Frey (Dorcas' sisters), the elated couple Dorcas
and me, Kerry (my brother), Richard Frede (a friend), Les Frey (Dorcas'
brother), and Bruce Toye (brother-in-law). Photos by Robert L. Barham

It was great to have the
blessings of our parents.
Ezra & Ada Frey graciously
received me into their family.
My mom, Muriel (Taylor)
Peterson, flew with Heather
and Kerry to be there for
our special day. She always
appreciated Dorcas until
the day she died.

Looking into
the eyes of the
love of my life,
Dorcas, for the
first time as
my dear wife.
She has been a
faithful
companion
and supporter
for over 36
years now.

Ready for another day at the canal. Working with sailors, as with all contacts, requires a lot of wisdom, holy boldness, Christlike love, and much prayer support.

An early family portrait. Our children are from left to right: Mark Andrew, Deborah Lynn, and Phillip Lawrence. Photo by Ian Ransberry

On the canal, I have the privilege of boarding ships from about 37 different countries whose sailors speak around 55 different languages. This particular ship I was aboard was from India.

Above: I am sitting in a dory that is similar to the one we used to have for my brothers and I to haul our lobster traps.

A model similar to my dad's long-liner was built by Hilton Chymist (pictured with me) whose father, Robert, gave me my first Bible.

I am recreating the memory of the final command from my dad as he said, "Cast off the lines Arthur." This time, it was for my brother, Ken, who is also a fishing captain.

Above: This quilt hanging from the ceiling in the Information Centre at Lockeport was made in memory of the 17 men who were lost at sea including my dad. Each man's face appears in the circles around the border. My dad is the centre one at the top.

My siblings and I all grown up. From left: Gordon, Arthur, Kerry, George, Ken, Heather, and John. All are married and have given Mom 23 grandchildren. There were 14 great-grandchildren at the time of her death. At the age of 78, my dear Mom, (Muriel Pomainville) prayed to receive Christ as her personal Saviour, so we are confident that she is in Heaven today.

Above: In all my 18 years of coaching baseball, Kelly Morris was the only girl on any of my teams. She is now my daughter-in-law (Mark's wife). She is third from the right in the front row beside our son Phil (second from right). Mark is on the far right in the back row.

Coaching our boys in baseball until they reached 21 years of age gave me the opportunity to make many new contacts with the boys and their parents. Many chances to be a blessing to them arose as we sought to maintain a Christlike example to them. Phil is second from the left, front row.

When Deborah was still quite a young girl I developed the habit of taking her on father-daughter dates. Here we went ice-skating. We became quite close as a result of these dates and we both have the love language of "touch".

Above: Our children managed to completely surprise us and arranged a renewal of our vows ceremony for us on our 30th anniversary in 1999. Mark posed as the officiator, Phil walked Dorcas down the aisle, Deborah was the matron of honour and one of the soloists. Our daughters-in-law Kelly and Katherine were bridesmaids, Phil was the best man and our son-in-law, Will Lewis, was a groomsman. Mark's daughter, Madison, and Deborah's daughter, Amanda, were the flower girls. They even arranged for our original soloist, Joyce Ruppert, to come and sing.

Parenting and then grandparenting, is something we always enjoyed. Since I liked babysitting my 6 siblings when I was just 11 years old, taking care of our grandchildren has become one of my favourite hobbies, so our children can have dates. Above left, Mikala and Jason come for a little cuddle time with Grampy. At right, Maegan is getting her first taste of Grampy's horsey back rides. She wasn't too sure at first but was soon laughing as I tossed her onto the couch after a round of the living room.

Above: The crew members of this 730 ft bulk carrier, the SCOTT MISENER, received me warmly. I was able to board her several times to give them some helpful marriage counsel and 2 of them accepted Christ as Saviour. Photo by Skip Gillham

Right: My cousin, Gordon West (on right), taught me how to box, which was another sport I got involved in during my high school years. He is with his wife, Donna (on left), and his mother, Marjorie West, who is my dad's sister.

I said "Farewell to Nova Scotia" but here we are, visiting back there and having a ride on my brother Ken's sailboat in the Shelburne harbour, touring the salmon farms.

Above: The Kissing Rock, at Lock Seven in Thorold, became famous as a spot where sailors would kiss their sweethearts good-bye before they boarded their ship in the Lock. I had the honour of performing the first wedding to take place at this location on July 1, 2005. John & Michelle Peach were fellow youth group members of our son Phil and his wife Katherine.

This is a different kind of family photo. My newly found sister, Hilda, is in the centre at the front. The five that aren't my siblings are her other 3 half-sisters and 2 half-brothers. Another half sister died of cancer a few years ago. Bringing these two families together makes her the eldest of 14 children. In the back row are her 2 brothers, Carl (on left), and Charlie Risser (third from left). In the front are the 3 sisters, Dorothy Longard (on left), Beverly Brine (next to Hilda on right), then Alvena McDonald (far right).

Above: A family photo taken on Christmas day 2004, shows how our family has expanded. Seated on the couch at left are Mark & Kelly's children Mitchell Lawrence, then twins Mikala Brook & Montanna Lee, and Madison Alexandra. Next are Deborah & Will's Jessica Faith and Amanda Grace. Behind them (right to left) in Will's arms is Jason William, Will, Deborah next to me. After Dorcas are Kelly & Mark and then Phil & Katherine with their Maegan Emily Day. Another baby is expected for them in March of 2006.

This family photo is of our unofficially adopted son, Jeff Hage, and his wife, Kari. The children are (left to right) Carter, Brock, Mallory, Taylor, and Peyton (in front). We are known as Gramma & Grampa "T" to them.

the couple was just not compatible so I suggested a six-month waiting period. Most couples, although not overjoyed, accepted my suggestion. However, in one situation the man became quite angry with me. After a period of time, his fiancee came to realize that he was not the right partner for her and she came to me and thanked me for the advice.

I became the sailors' taxi driver to the store, bank and union hall, and sometimes their mail carrier. These opportunities gave me a chance to show them the practical side of the Christian life. I didn't want them to see me only as a preacher talking Christianity and not living it.

I would visit the union hall's parking lot to talk with sailors who were out of work and waiting for job postings. Some of these seamen became very discouraged because they did not have a job and could not support their family. I would take them to a restaurant, buy them a good meal, and try to tell them about the Lord who cares about them and wants to meet their every need.

On sadder occasions, I would go and visit a few sailors who were in prison for various crimes. I couldn't change their circumstances, but I would mail their letters or visit their family. I would try and encourage them to see that God could forgive any sin and give them a new life with a wonderful purpose.

One incident affected me tremendously and altered my approach to troubled seamen. A sailor came into conflict with some captains and union officials. He was 'kicked' out of the union because he had started his own home-based business on the side to support his family. It wasn't just any business, though.

He would loan money at a high interest rate. At the same time, he ran a prostitution ring and sold drugs. The police uncovered the operation and many were charged, but not this individual sailor. He managed to cover up his involvement, but as a result, all his friends turned against him.

He became despondent. I managed to meet him and we struck up a friendship. We both were from Nova Scotia and had an extensive background in fishing. He told me he was broke and missed his family back in Cape Breton. He also explained, "The police are still after me and I am desperate for help."

As he was telling me his life story, I glanced at my watch and saw that I was late for a baseball game at our chapel that I helped organize every week. I should have phoned someone there to fill in for me, but instead, I told this sailor that I had to go and that I would arrange to see him again the next day.

That night, he was involved in a high speed police chase, rolled his car and was killed. I felt awful! Here was a sinner lost and headed for hell. I asked the Lord to forgive me and I made it a point not to put "self" on the throne. This was a hard lesson to learn.

My responsibilities have also come to include helping sailors and their family members through grief in the loss of a loved one. This isn't the easiest task. If someone dies without knowing Christ as their Saviour and Lord, it is difficult explaining to anyone who asks that they are not in Heaven. I have to make it very clear that these are God's words in the Bible, not mine. As well, by nature, I'm always wearing a smile. I think God increased it when I was saved. Some families have been upset with me because I'm always smiling during a solemn and serious funeral service. I am learning to be more discrete during these times.

When the canal is shut down for the winter months, I travel to various gatherings of God's people to tell them of the work on the canal. These visits can take me all over Ontario and to the border states of the United States. I generally put about sixty-five thousand kilometers a year on my vehicle. My work for the Lord does involve long hours on the road and being away from home.

While my service has not been perfect, I'm always aware what God has said in His Word that *"all things work together for good to them that love God"* (Romans 8:28). This is never more evident than when I see the sovereign hand of God act in the most miraculous ways.

CHAPTER FOURTEEN

God's Miraculous Hand

It is easy to fall into the trap of thinking that you are the most important person in a ministry, that the work of the Lord wouldn't succeed without you. The Bible states that we are to acknowledge all our ways before Him and only then will He direct our path. This is my goal, then— to allow God to work through me in such a way that He will get all the glory. Not everything has worked out perfectly in the thirty-three years I've been on the Canal. I have gone months without seeing a soul saved, and have driven many miles to help someone only to be unsuccessful. However, I am constantly being encouraged by seeing the hand of God at work.

I once boarded a ship from Ghana, West Africa. I soon began to receive a lot of persecution. One sailor took a New Testament that I offered to him, spit on it and threw it overboard. He was so upset, so anti-Christian. I quietly asked God to help me show him love and mercy. I just smiled, turned and walked away without saying a word. I went down to the recreation room where I left "card talks" for all the sailors on board. These cards are a piece of waxed cardboard with a little record needle. You put a pen in a hole near the centre of the record and rotate it. A message can be heard as you regulate the speed. What these men were hearing was a Gospel message in their own language. To the men on the ship, this was like a free toy to play with.

The man that threw my New Testament overboard later wrote me a letter and told me he was curious why I didn't get angry with him and why I had left those 'toy record cards' with total strangers. He was curious about the message on the record so he played it, heard the Gospel and was saved. He also played it for his wife and children and they, too, trusted the Lord as their Saviour. He told other sailors about what had happened to him and to his family. The result was that many other sailors trusted Christ. Within three years, more than three hundred people became believers in the Lord Jesus back in his country. A missionary then came and set up a local church in their hometown of Takoradi. God uses individuals from every walk of life to accomplish His purposes.

I have also learned that, despite 'my' plans and becoming disappointed in not having things work out the way I want, God has His own timetable. I was invited to speak at a chapel in Sault Ste. Marie in Northern Ontario. I couldn't go on the day they requested so I agreed to an earlier date. After speaking on the Sunday, I was eager to return home the next day to see my family but God had a different plan.

As I was preparing to leave Monday morning, I was asked to stay another day so I could visit a local jail to speak to the inmates that evening. Many of these were recovering drug addicts and alcoholics. Although no one put their trust in the Lord, the Gospel was well received and I was very encouraged by their listening ear.

Early Tuesday morning as I was getting ready to leave, I received an emergency phone call from a believer who explained that there was a crisis at the local shipping lock. A cruise ship company from Greece had gone bankrupt. It had flown the officers back home to Greece, but had left twenty deck hands stranded, with no food, money or a place to stay. It was suggested that I might want to go and check out the situation.

When I arrived, some of the sailors were in a fowl mood, swearing and cursing at whoever was in authority. They wanted to return back home to their families. I reached into my pocket and offered them all the money I had, about thirty-five dollars. They began to mock me and said, "Oh! Here is the Chaplain! He is giving us thirty-five dollars to fly the twenty of us back to Greece." I smiled and said that I knew of a friend, David Mulholland in Toronto, who helped sailors who were in a desperate way. I made the call and arrangements were made to drive these sailors to Windsor, Ontario, which was the closest airport. There each sailor was given a free ticket back home. Needless to say, they were very thankful. But the story does not end there.

A few months later as I boarded a ship from Greece in the Canal, I talked to a very upset sailor. The ship had broken down and he was not going to get home to see his family for quite some time. He said, "Religion hasn't solved my problems and I am angry at God." He asked me who I was and what I did. I said, "I am Arthur Taylor, the Chaplain for the Welland Canal." "Oh," he replied, "I've heard about you. My buddies back home told me how you helped them get back to their families after being stranded in Canada. Their wives and children were so happy for what you did." His attitude suddenly softened and he listened to me as I told him how Christ died for his sins and could give him peace and purpose in his life. Right there, he placed his faith in the Lord Jesus Christ.

Two other incidents drove home the fact to me that God's timing is perfect. I was in Toronto helping my daughter, Deborah, and her husband, Will Lewis. They were having car problems. I was scheduled to meet a troubled sailor who was getting off his ship at a port in Clarkson, about a forty-five minute drive from Toronto. I had given myself plenty of time to do what I had to do, however, events took longer than I anticipated. Still thinking

I could make it, I got in the car and headed down the highway.

Thirty minutes down the road, a major chemical oil spill had occurred and everything was blocked off. Toronto rush hour traffic had come to a dead stop in all directions. After sitting there for an hour or so, I decided to try a different route. This would literally make me three hours late, but I had given my word to this sailor that I would be there for him.

I arrived at the dock and found, to my surprise, the ship had run into problems and was three hours late as well, and was to arrive shortly. I was actually early! The sailor was very apologetic for being so late. As I told him my story in trying to get to the port on time, he was impressed by the fact that I would keep my word and not treat my work as a '9 to 5' job. He was in awe of how God had directed both of our events that day. He got in my car and we ran a few errands. I shared the Gospel with him and, before long, he placed his faith in Christ.

On another occasion, I was riding a ship through the canal and became very involved in talking with a group of sailors, so much so that I missed getting off at my usual stop. I now had to go to the next lock in order to get off. As I jumped off the ship, I saw a crowd of excited tourists looking at a ledge that was just below a lock. As I got closer, I saw why everyone was alarmed. There was a young teenage girl sitting on the ledge, ready to jump into the canal and commit suicide. She had warned the crowd to stay back, but I decided to get as close as I could without scaring her in order to talk to her. She yelled, "Stay away!"

I replied, "Okay. I'll just sit here." I asked her, "What is so terrible in your life that you would want to end it?"

She told me, "My dad has abandoned me and my mom is an alcoholic. I've lost my part-time job, I didn't make the softball team, I'm doing poorly at school, but worst of all, my boyfriend left me for someone else." She looked at me and said sadly, "Life is not worth living."

I tried talking with her: "I can't solve all your problems. I can't bring your father or your boyfriend back, and if your mother doesn't want help, I can't do anything about that. But, I am sure I know someone who can give you a part-time job, and I do know of a girl's softball team who is looking for players your age." She paused for a moment and then carefully got up. I gently took her by the arm and led her away from the ledge.

I made arrangements for her to get some needed help and to stay at her girlfriend's house. I was able to secure her a job and then helped her join a local girl's softball team. I visited her over the coming weeks and gave her some Gospel literature. I arranged for her to attend a local ladies' Bible study group that was going through the book, "Lord, Heal My Hurts." I encouraged her to attend a 'Youth for Christ' meeting in a high school. It was at that meeting that she turned her life over to the Lord and trusted in His finished work on the cross.

Through all of these experiences, and many others, I'm left amazed that God delights to use me in His mighty work of reaching lost souls. The qualities that I had often thought were my weaknesses have turned out to be the very means through which God has proven His power. I've had to learn, first-hand, the truth of 2 Corinthians 12:9, *"My grace is sufficient for thee: for my strength is made perfect in weakness.*

Most gladly therefore will I rather glory in my infirmities, that the power of Christ may rest upon me." However, it has often been through humbling experiences that the Lord has taught me this important lesson.

CHAPTER FIFTEEN

The Person God Uses

As I've mentioned already, there are fifty-five languages represented on the ships in the Welland Canal. If you were the boss of a company, would you pick someone like me, who had failed English in high school and doesn't really express himself too well publicly, to be your spokesperson? I don't think so. Even more importantly, would you pick me to present the most life-changing message in the world, the Gospel of Jesus Christ? Again I would doubt it very much. But that is just the point:

"God hath chosen the foolish things of the world to confound the wise; and God hath chosen the weak things of the world to confound the things which are mighty; And base things of the world, and things which are despised,

hath God chosen, yea, and things which are not, to bring to nought things that are: That no flesh should glory in his presence" (1 Corinthians 1:27-29).

Here is one example of how my weakness in English has turned out for God's glory. Every ship has a radio officer. He must be able to speak English as well as his country's language on the ship. His duties mainly include speaking with the Seaway Authority as the ship is entering the canal and maintaining contact after the ship enters a port. While the ship is in the canal, though, he is usually off duty. Most radio officers on the ships happily agree to help me.

Take, for example, an Italian ship entering the canal. I would jump on board and give the radio officer an Italian Bible. We would make our way throughout the ship, talking to sailors. I would read a verse in English and he would read it in Italian. I would make comments in English and he would interpret them in Italian. He would take their questions in Italian and tell them to me in English, and so on. He soon would get to know my message, word for word, and speak it with such enthusiasm, even better than me. See the wisdom and ways of a sovereign God: Here you have a lost sinner preaching to

THE PERSON GOD USES

his lost buddies and some of them trusting Christ as their Saviour! After doing this several times around his ship, the radio officer memorized the verse in Acts 16:31 – *"Believe on the Lord Jesus Christ and thou shalt be saved."* He came to me and wanted to pray to get saved. God works in mysterious ways.

Another example of whom God may use is when, from my human perspective, my canal ministry seemed to be in jeopardy. The St. Lawrence Seaway Authority issues only one pass a year for a chaplain to ride the ships. To date, the Welland Canal Mission has received it for 137 years. A certain member of a religious group which believes there are many roads leading to Heaven objected to this procedure, stating it was favoring one religion over another. He asked the Ministry of Transportation official (who was attending the dedication ceremony of the new by-pass for the canal) that the Seaway Authority change their position and give his religious group a turn on the ships.

The government official agreed to have a meeting with this individual to examine the issue. Initially, I was not invited but later was granted permission to attend. After a lengthy discussion, it was opened for comments from some Seaway workers who had also been at the canal on the opening day. I wrestled with the idea of saying something or remaining silent. I decided it was the Lord's work, not mine. I would silently pray and watch His hand work.

Suddenly, one man from the Seaway Authority stood up and said, "The Welland Canal Mission does not believe in suing." I had met with a Seaway official when I first started on the ships and explained to him that I don't believe in suing. The reason was simply that, if I did sue the Seaway Authority, they would not be very happy with me and I would lose their listening ear. I then couldn't obey the verse in Mark 16:15 – *"Go ye into all the world and preach the gospel to EVERY creature."* He agreed with that logic and said, "We love that kind of religion."

A linesman rose to his feet and said, "The Welland Canal Mission has never asked for one cent from anybody, not from sailors or from the Seaway Authority in 137 years." Then a Lock Master said, "The Welland Canal Missionaries love us and have been a real help to sailors and our government workers in providing counselling and performing marriages for free." The government official then declined the proposal from the religious group and stated that it would be the Welland Canal Mission or nobody to be the 'religious representative' on the ships. I said nothing, but silently I praised God for His all-powerful ways.

All of these experiences draw out my heart in worship to the sovereign God, as His will is being accomplished through me in the many different circumstances of life. This truth strengthens me when I often find myself in unusual situations. I am actually a *"labourer together with God"* (1 Corinthians 3:9). It also challenges me to just make myself available to Him and obey His Word, His way and His will so that He might get the honour, praise and glory.

As I draw my reflections to a close, starting from a troubled teenager who lacked any sense of real purpose in life, to a servant of the Lord with a glorious calling, permit me to explain God's message of love to you. Just as it changed my life, so it can change yours.

CHAPTER SIXTEEN

Lost at Sea,
Found in Heaven

M y story has covered over fifty years of my life. Much of the journey has been filled with incidents that God allowed in order to help me realize that He loves me and has a plan for my life. In this last chapter, I would again like to emphasize that plan, the greatest life-changing experience a person can know.

When I was a youth of twelve or thirteen, my mother started a Sunday School in the local church building. A lady by the name of Rita Swim helped her by reading Bible stories to us. Months later when she finished the book, and since there were no other books available, Sunday School as we knew it ended. I was sorry that those times were over. It left me with a lot of questions, but no answers, wanting more information, but finding none.

Six or seven years later, I found out that there was indeed more to the Bible and it was then I discovered the greatest news in the world. This news totally revolutionized my life. I found out that my so-called 'exciting' country-boy lifestyle, motives, attitudes and actions, in comparison with God's standards, revealed that I was a sinner. God's holiness and His true and righteous law proved that I was sinning against God. I did indeed have a sin nature and could do nothing about it, no matter how hard I might try or how religious I could be. I had assumed that since I had never robbed the Lockeport Bank, caused a girl to become pregnant, or murdered any-one, I was an OK guy and my love for people would get me into Heaven if I were to die.

I discovered that Christ said in the Bible that my present position before the God of Heaven was that I was a lost sinner under His judgment (see John 3:36). He hates sin, and sin cannot enter Heaven or it wouldn't be Heaven. I found out that it was a sin to lust after women, steal people's apples from their orchards, and break hunting and fishing laws. I read in the Bible that the laws and authorities are ordained of God. I was guilty of all of the above and more.

I found out that the Bible taught that, in this state, I was a lost sinner and needed to be saved to enter into Heaven. Humanly speaking, I could relate this to my dad's final experience at sea. When the fierce winter storm struck, he was fifty miles from shore in his fishing vessel. All his efforts to save himself were helpless and his cries for help on the ship to shore radio were silenced by the angry waves. The storm had come up so suddenly and, before he knew it, he was staring death in the face. He needed someone with a larger ship to come to his rescue and save him and his crew. He was a good man and loved his family and his crew members but that couldn't save him. He was hopelessly lost at sea.

Here is the Good News! In Luke 19:10, Jesus says, *"For the Son of man is come to seek and to save that which was lost."* In my situation, I had agreed with God that I was a sinner, lost in my sins, and had no power to stop sinning in order to meet His perfect standards. It was a great relief to me when I realized that I didn't have to somehow reach up to God and try to pull myself up to meet Him to get His approval. He was seeking me and wanted to save me, *"He is not willing that any should perish"* (2 Peter 3:9). How could Jesus save me?

The holy God of Heaven came to this earth as the baby Jesus, *"And she shall bring forth a son, and thou shalt call His name Jesus: for He shall save His people from their sins"* (Matthew 1:21). He could not sin and thus He was qualified to take on the penalty for all my sins— the death penalty. He did this when He died on the cross. *"But God commendeth His love toward us, in that, while we were yet sinners, Christ died for us"* (Romans 5:8).

An illustration of this is when a person agrees with a Judge that he has committed a crime. The Judge passes judgment and says that the punishment is either $100,000 or 10 years in jail. He doesn't have the money so he is hopelessly lost and headed for the jail term. However, a rich friend comes along and pays the fine for him. The Judge has accepted the money and the guilty man is set free and can go in peace. In the same way, Jesus paid my debt as a sinner, *"While we were yet sinners Christ died for us"* (Romans 5:8).

I heard a sermon that explained how we know that the Bible is true. One reason is that all the facts told about Christ in the Old Testament before He was born were fulfilled 100% during His life here on earth, His death and His resurrection. I decided to say, "God said it, I believe it, and that settles it." What do I have to do to benefit from all that God has done for me? Simply, *"Believe on the Lord Jesus Christ and you will be SAVED"* (Acts 16:31).

I was shown Romans 10:9, *"That if thou shalt confess with thy mouth the Lord Jesus, and shalt believe in thine heart that God hath raised Him from the dead, thou shalt be SAVED."* I just had to believe in my heart that Jesus died on the cross to pay for all my sins and that He rose again on the third day, and thereby, made it possible for Him to become my Saviour.

Another verse that was used in helping me to come to my faith in Christ was John 3:16. I was told to read it with my name in it. It read like this, *"For God so loved **Arthur** that He gave His only begotten Son (Jesus); that if **Arthur** would believe in Him, **Arthur** would not perish but **Arthur** would have everlasting life."* I thanked Him for taking my penalty upon Himself, for conquering sin and death and for rising again from the dead. I asked Him by faith to be my personal Saviour and to save me. As soon as I did that, my guilt was gone. I had instant peace. Shortly after this, He started changing my life from the inside out as I learned more truth about Him and was willing to accept His help in obeying His truths. An inner joy filled my life that I had never before experienced in this world. I was then shown another Bible truth. John 1:12 says *"But as many as received Him, to them He gives the power (or right) to become the children of God."* I had just become a child of God.

Here is an illustration that might help explain this truth. My mother would work hard shearing the sheep, picking the dirt out of the wool, washing and drying it, and then shipping it away to be spun and dyed. This latter process also cost money and we weren't rich. She then spent hours knitting this wool into sweaters, mittens, and socks, putting each of the seven children's name on the item so we wouldn't get them mixed up. Mom would then put them all under the tree for a Christmas gift for each of us. Although she worked hard to get them there, they were free to us. The work was all done. I couldn't knit. I just had to believe that it was mine. She loved me and wanted me to have it. All I had to do was to reach under the tree and claim the free gift as mine in order to benefit from her labour of love. Letting it sit under the tree would not keep me warm. I had to believe that it was mine and take it and wear it.

In the same way, Jesus did all the work for me, but it wouldn't have done me any good if I didn't receive His free gift of salvation for myself. Once I received it, I could claim the verse in John 5:24, *"Verily, verily I say unto you, He that heareth my word, and believeth on Him that sent me, HATH everlasting life, and SHALL NOT come into condemnation but IS passed from death unto life (spiritually)."* Another verse of assurance is found in I John 5:13 – *"These things have I written unto you that believe on the name of the Son of God that ye may KNOW that ye have eternal life."* WOW! I certainly don't deserve this but, because of Jesus Christ, I am guaranteed eternal life. The date of my spiritual birth is January 23, 1966. It was that Sunday evening in Lockeport, Nova Scotia, and it was the best thing that ever happened to me.

My dad was in Heaven! Years later, in the spring of 1998, the Lord gave me the privilege of helping my mom understand God's love for her and she made a personal decision to trust Christ as her Lord and Saviour. Her dear Lord called her home to Glory on ay

September 24, 2004. What a reunion we will have as we will all be FOUND IN HEAVEN some day! I hope and pray that ALL my family, including extended relatives, as well as friends and those who read this book, will make this same decision. It's my prayer that you won't wait to do this. The Bible says, *"TODAY is the day of salvation"* because *"....your life is like a vapour that appeareth for a little time, and then vanisheth away."* (James 4:14b). Do it now before it is too late.

As I look back now, I see how God was able to bring good out of that fishing disaster. I feel humbled and honoured to have a little part in God's plan. God sees the total picture. He allowed the disaster, He didn't cause it! He picked up the pieces after he had people's listening ear. The Bible says that, *"Faith comes by hearing, and hearing by the word of God"* (Romans 10:17). He sure caught my listening ear. I may never have gone on to study to be a Chaplain if Dad had been around. But now I have the privilege of sharing God's plan of eternal life with sailors from thirty-seven different countries as well as those around Lockeport when I go home for a visit. The Bible also says that, *"All things work together for good to them that love God, to them who are called according to His purpose"* (Romans 8:28). I have found His purpose. Have you?

Epilogue

The previous chapter is the most important part of the book and I would suggest that you pause here and read it over again very carefully and thoughtfully and consider if you can relate to any of this. Christ says in His Word that *"narrow is the way, which leadeth unto life, and few there be that find it"* (Matthew 7:14). I pray you will be one of those who find it. He also said, *"I am the way the truth and the life. No one comes to the Father but by Me"* (John 14:6).

There are eight children in our family and all but Hilda and I still live in Nova Scotia. She lives near Gravenhurst, Ontario. Hilda discovered some time ago that she was a Taylor by birth and, in a long and interesting journey, made herself known to the rest of us about five years ago. But that story would take another whole chapter to tell. She has added a new and happy dimension to our lives and finally – a sister for our Heather. So in order of birth, we are: Hilda, Arthur, Kerry, Ken, John, Gordon, George, and Heather.

As for my immediate family, my story would not be complete without sharing my dear wife Dorcas' background and emphasizing how important she has been to me and the work of the Welland Canal Mission.

Dorcas Frey was born into a family where God was worshipped and taught, both in the home and in their local assembly. Her parents, Ezra and Ada Frey, were raised in Waterloo County, Ontario, as Old Order Mennonites, getting around by horse and buggy. They both found that a personal relationship with Jesus Christ was necessary in order to have the assurance that they would go to Heaven when they die. So they left the Mennonites and helped to form a local assembly in Hawkesville, Ontario, which is now known as Wallenstein Bible Chapel. The Lord blessed them with five children. In order of birth they are: Esther, Dorcas (Taylor), Amos, Marlene (Toye) and Les. Sadly, Amos was taken to Heaven when he was just nineteen months old.

Dorcas' parents instilled into their children, from an early age, a great interest in mission work. As a result, all four surviving children have, at some time or other, served the Lord in a full-time capacity.

One day, a missionary to Uruguay, South America came to visit the Freys. His name was Dr. Hamilton and he asked Dorcas if she had asked the Lord Jesus to be her Saviour. She was nine years old at the time and acknowledged that she had not placed her faith in the Lord. This caused Dorcas' heart to become very unsettled and, the following week, she asked her dad to help her. Interestingly enough, her dad used the same verse in the same way that I had been challenged to do. He had Dorcas insert her name into John 3:16 as well, and she trusted Christ as Lord and Saviour.

Dorcas graduated as a registered nurse at the age of twenty-two in Cambridge, Ontario. It was also around this time that she attended a weekend Youth Retreat in Guelph, Ontario. Under the ministry of Keith Price, she rededicated her life to serve the Lord wherever He would lead. After working in her hospital as an RN for one year, she then spent the next three years at Emmaus Bible School. The following three years she was employed as a full-time nurse at

Moody Bible Institute. It was here that Dorcas and I would cross paths for the first time. She usually explains it this way: "A handsome, outgoing young student who was on fire for God came under my care and I've been taking care of him ever since!"

The Lord has blessed us with three children. Our oldest boy, Mark, married Kelly Morris on July 31, 1993, and they live in St. Catharines with their four children, Madison (10), Mitchell (7), and twins Mikala and Montanna (5). Our daughter, Deborah, married Will Lewis on July 2, 1994 and they reside in Prince Edward Island along with their three children, Amanda (9), Jessica (8) and Jason (4). Our youngest son, Phillip, was married to Katherine Wright on August 22, 1998 and they make their home in Waterloo, Ontario with their two daughters Maegan (2) and Lauren Rebecca Elizabeth, born March 7, 2006.

We also took in a teenager named Jeff Hage, whom we have come to love as a son and who now affectionately calls us 'Mom' and 'Dad'. He lived with us periodically for twelve years until he got married. He met his wife Kari Mysak at Emmaus Bible College and they were married on May 25, 1995. Their home is in New York and they have five children, Taylor (7), Carter (6), Peyton (4), Brock (3) and Mallory (1). They call us "Grandma and Grandpa T". So the present count for grandchildren stands at thirteen with the fourteenth expected.

To write how my dear wife has been a helpmate to me in the ministry of the Welland Canal Mission would take a book in itself. However, it must be emphasized that she has been fully committed to this work and we have really worked as one. This is very important—let it serve as a challenge to those couples who seek to serve the Lord, that both must be willing to enter a work for the Lord and be prepared to accept the blessings as well as the hardships and difficulties you will encounter.

We covet your prayers as God still sees fit to use us for His glory. Upon reviewing the details of our journey, there is only one thing that we can say, *"To the only wise God our Saviour, be glory and majesty, dominion and power, both now and ever. Amen"* (Jude 1:25).

Lost At Sea, Found in Heaven may have raised questions you would like answered. If so, please e-mail Arthur Taylor at **dorcas.taylor@sympatico.ca** OR **wcmission@sympatico.ca** You can also contact Bob Cretney at **bobcretney@hotmail.com**

Dedication

I would like to dedicate this book to all the people who played a major spiritual role in my life:

To Judy (Williams) Kohler, who agreed to be my date and took me to her church service where I heard the gospel for the first time. This led to my salvation experience.

To Pastor Eustace Marshall, who led me to become a true, born again believer and thus inherit eternal life in Heaven.

To Robert Chymist, who gave me my first Bible and challenged me to make it my authority, my direction and my wisdom in life.

To Robert Dabb, who befriended me as a stranger in Jersey City and took me to a revival meeting. It was there that I went forward to dedicate my whole life a living sacrifice to God (Romans 12:1) and to obey Mark 16:15 in response to a missions challenge.

To Luis and Lydia Muniz, who introduced me to Robert Dabb and have regularly kept in touch with me in encouragement and financial support to the present.

To Vic Williams, who made a statement to Pryor Stewart, a Christian teacher at my high school. And to Pryor, who then included that statement in his letter to the registrar: "God has his hand on Arthur, and you should seriously consider him as a student. He is a 'diamond in the rough'." Without this, I may not have been accepted.

To Dr. Wm. Culbertson, who was the president of Moody Bible Institute and who took special time in helping me to learn the application of Romans 6 into my life so that sin would not have dominion over me.

To Sumner Wemp, who was the head of the Evangelism Department at Moody. The comments he would make between the verses of the song,

Make Me a Blessing, were truly led of the Holy Spirit. They inspired us to become emptied of ourselves and to allow our loving Saviour to pour His love through us to others.

To Dean Robert Irvin, who was an encouragement to me in many ways while I was a student at Moody Bible Institute and who was God's instrument in introducing me to Cameron Orr and the ministry of the Welland Canal Mission.

To Cameron Orr, who had the faith to believe that I was God's man to succeed him.

To "Uncle Dave" Stiefler, who taught me the principle of learning when to get out of the way and let God do His work in His way with His Word.

To Sam Learning, who taught me the wisdom of seeing the 'lostness of the lost' and developing a Christlike compassion for them.

To Valerie Hall, who has asked for prayer requests and has literally prayed for me and my family daily for over 30 years.

To Don Hill, who influenced me to make Jesus Christ my 'Everything'.

To Margaret Broderick, whom I met in my first years when she was a cook on the ships. The Lord allowed me to have a part in her salvation and then she became my 'adopted mother' in the home port upon her retirement and to this day.

To Audrey Douglas, Bea Axford, Joy Hill, Jean Bartley, Gladys Carey, Ruth Abbott, Dorothy Walker, Doris Greenhow, Verna Manson, Norma Alguire, Florence Ricketts, and Marlene Toye, who all willingly and lovingly served me meals and housing at least a week each year when I was visiting contacts in their community. This freed me up to grow spiritually through serving others. Some of them did this for as many as 20 to 30 years.

And locally, Bill Sanders and Tom Bacon and their wives, who faithfully for over 30 years have taken a personal interest in how we are doing as a family and how I am coping with all the stress that is involved in working with sailors in crisis.

Also, Wendell DeVries and Kevin Downs, who

have kept my vehicle running and given me helpful materials so I could be a blessing to others.

And now to the one whom God has seen fit to give me as my help meet. My dear wife, Dorcas, has stood by my side through 36 years of marriage and service for the Lord. She has always supported me and prayed for me. God even gave her peace about our call into this ministry before He gave it to me! However, as a submissive wife, she didn't tell me about it until I expressed to her what I felt was God's leading regarding the ministry to the sailors.

As long as the children were still at home, she was content to stay with them so that I would be free to minister without being concerned for them. She is always a willing partner in whatever undertakings I might propose. Besides doing all the secretarial and accounting duties, she also edits all my writings to make sure that correct grammar is used and that the spiritual message is properly conveyed. A good example is this book. Dorcas has laboured tirelessly in the editing and re-editing of this project, along with Bob Cretney, Brian Cretney, and John Nicholson. With her help, my thoughts came through as I expressed them, though it meant many long hours into the nights—or right through the nights—just to meet deadlines. My dear wife also offers wise advice to keep me on the straight and narrow, so that I might refrain from giving even the slightest 'appearance of evil'.

Most of all, I dedicate this book to my loving Heavenly Father. I pray that He might get all the glory for what HE has done in taking a poor and sinful fisherman, saving him, then sending him out to be a fisher of men to further His kingdom. To God be the glory!